WHO WOULD WIN?®

WOLVERINE

VS.

TASMANIAN DEVIL

BY
JERRY PALLOTTA
ILLUSTRATED BY
ROB BOLSTER

Scholastic Inc.

The publisher would like to thank the following for their
kind permission to use their photographs in this book:

Page 20: © Lupa; page 21: © Jurgen & Christine Sohns / FLPA;
page 23: © Soren Andersson / WpN / Photoshot; page 26: top: © Daniel J. Cox /
Photographer's Choice / Getty Images; bottom: © Chris Klingler;
page 27: top: © Alecia Carter / ARKive; bottom: © Dave Watts / Visuals Unlimited, Inc.

To my pal Mark O'Connor . . . I have never heard of Mike Leonard.
—J.P.

To the Westwood Massachusetts High School Wolverines and Coach Russell Downes.
—R.B.

ISBN 978-93-5471-032-2

10 9 8 7 6 5 4 3 2 1 20 21 22 23 24

This reprint edition : September 2024
Printed in India at : VK Global Digital Private Limited

What would happen if a wolverine came face-to-face with a Tasmanian devil? What if they had a fight? Who do you think would win?

SCIENTIFIC NAME OF WOLVERINE: "Gulo gulo"

Meet the wolverine. Its scientific name means "glutton." A glutton is someone who eats a lot.

DEFINITION
A mammal is a warm-blooded animal with fur that gives milk to its young.

NICKNAMES
Skunk Bear, Nasty Cat, Carcajou, Quick Hatch, Gulon, and Mountain Cat.

Wolverines are mammals. A wolverine is not a small wolf. It is in the weasel class of animals. A wolverine grows to be about three feet long, and weigh up to 40 pounds.

SCIENTIFIC NAME OF TASMANIAN DEVIL: "Sarcophilus harrisii"

Meet the Tasmanian devil. Its scientific name means "flesh lover."

DEFINITION
A marsupial is a mammal that carries its young in a pouch.

NICKNAMES
The Taz, the Butcher, Bear Devil.

A Tasmanian devil is a type of mammal called a marsupial. It grows to be two and a half feet long and weigh up to 25 pounds.

ANIMALS IN THE WEASEL FAMILY

ferret

cuscus

honey badger

FACT

The sea mink is an extinct weasel.

marten

DID YOU KNOW?

Wolverines do not hibernate.

least weasel

STRANGE FACT

At one time, people thought a wolverine was the runt of a bear litter.

OTHER MARSUPIALS

kangaroo

koala

RARE FACT
A yapok is an aquatic marsupial that lives in South America.

wallaby

wombat

THINK!
Can you think of another animal that begins with Q?

Page 32 has answers.

quoll

FACT
The Tasmanian wolf is an extinct marsupial.

NORTHERN HEMISPHERE

Wolverines live in cold climates, such as North America, Northern Asia, and Northern Europe. Wolverines love mountains, snow, ice, and glaciers.

FACT

In deep snow, a wolverine has an advantage over prey that have hooves. Wolverine feet are wide.

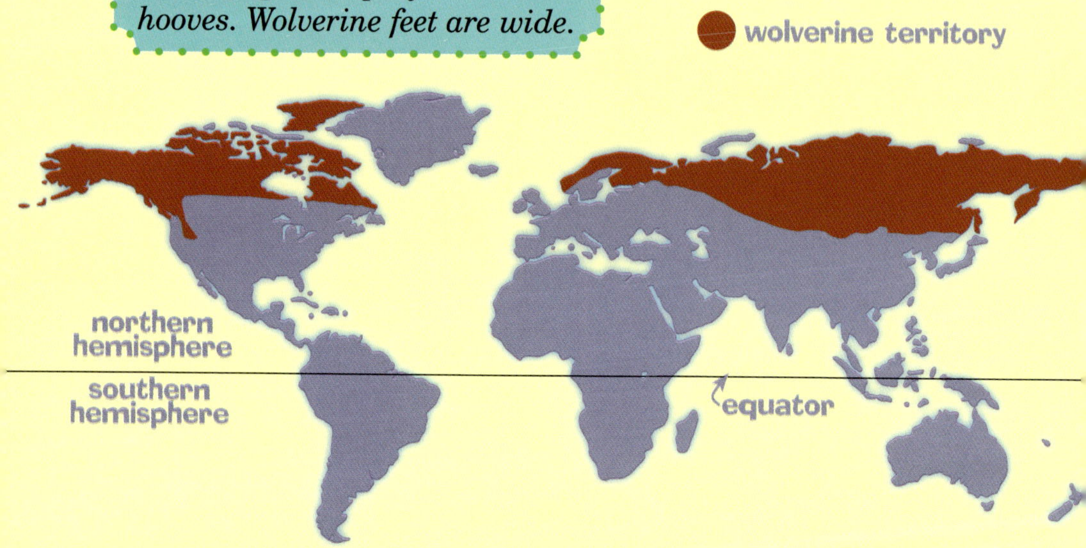

COLLEGE FACT

The University of Michigan teams call themselves the Wolverines.

DID YOU KNOW?

There are no wolverines in the southern hemisphere.

TASMANIA

Tasmanian devils live in Tasmania. Tasmania is an island off the southeast coast of Australia. They live in coastal scrubland and eucalyptus forests.

DID YOU KNOW?
Australia is 90 percent desert.

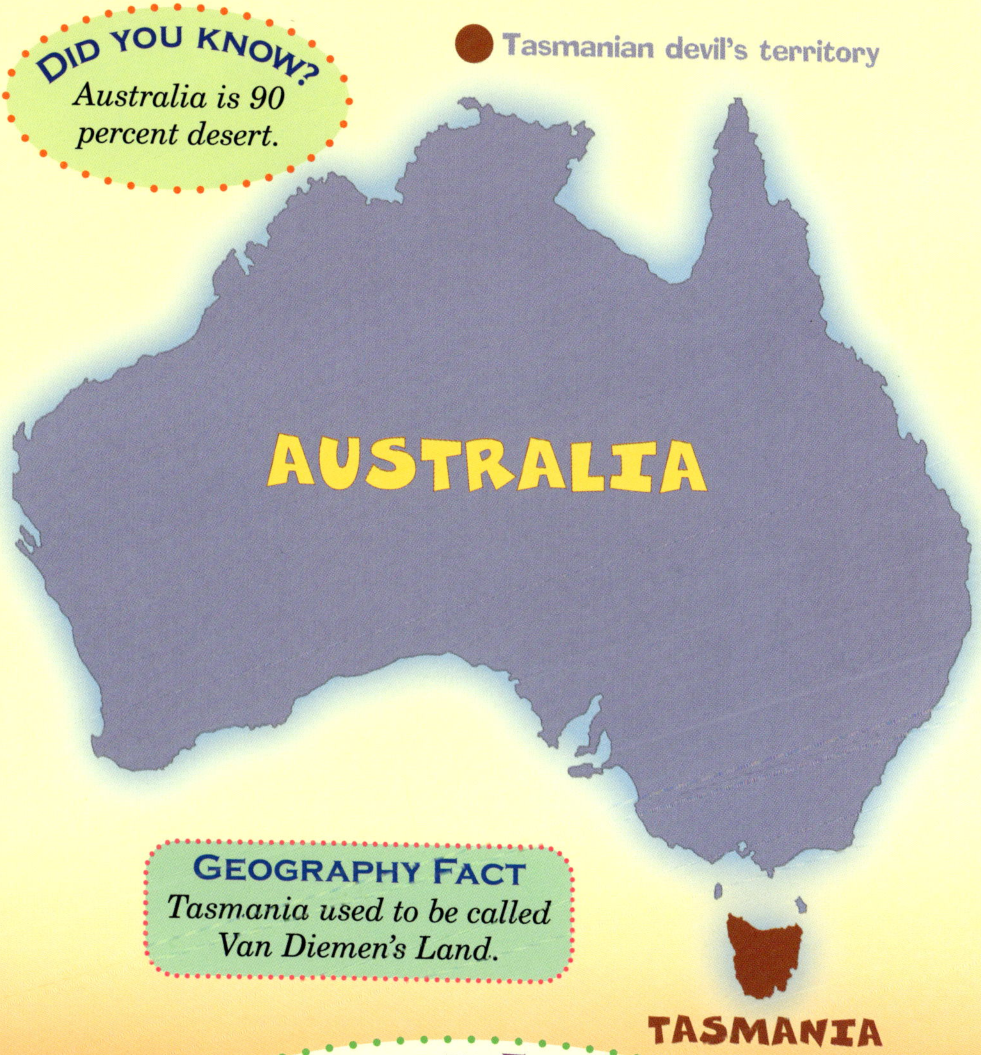

GEOGRAPHY FACT
Tasmania used to be called Van Diemen's Land.

SPORTS FACT
A soccer team from Bellerive, Tasmania, called itself the Tasmanian Devils Football Club.

WOLVERINE ADJECTIVES

brutal
tenacious
ferocious
solitary
merciless
mysterious
elusive
powerful
volatile
determined

GOOD IDEA

Get a dictionary and look up these words!

DID YOU KNOW?
People have seen grizzly bears walk away from a wolverine.

TASMANIAN DEVIL DESCRIPTIONS

loud

vicious

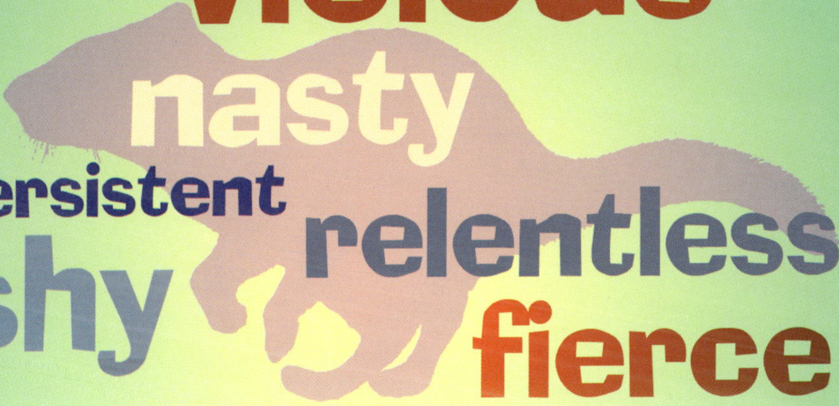

nasty

persistent

relentless

shy

fierce

ANOTHER GOOD IDEA

Remember how to spell these words!

CHALLENGE!
Get a thesaurus and look up similar words.

TEETH

Here is the skull of a wolverine. No one wants to get bitten by a wolverine. Look at the back teeth—they are perfect for crushing bones.

AMAZING FACT
These animals live on different continents but their skulls are incredibly similar.

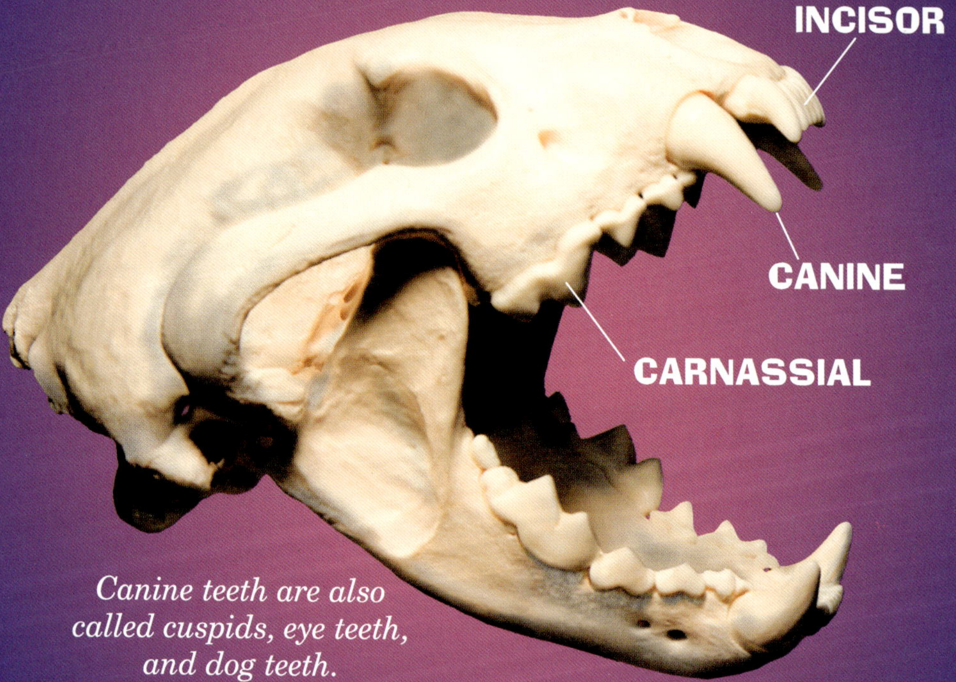

Canine teeth are also called cuspids, eye teeth, and dog teeth.

DID YOU KNOW?
A carnassial tooth is shaped for cutting and scraping meat.

FUN FACT
Few people have ever kept an adult wolverine for a pet.

JAWS

Here is the skull of a Tasmanian devil. When they bite, they don't like to let go.

DENTAL FACT
Humans have no carnassials.

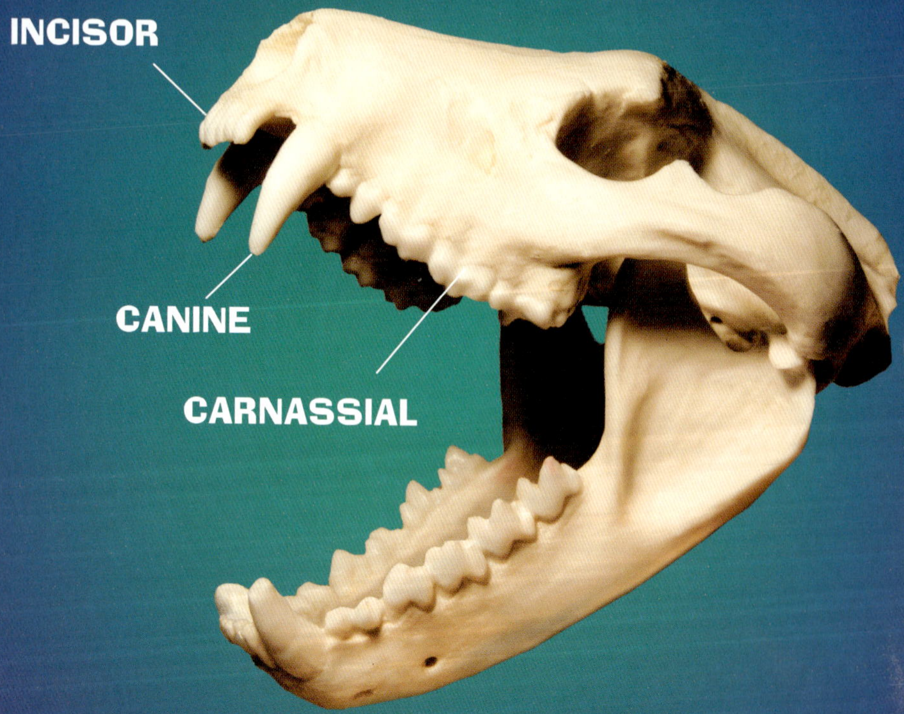

Look at its jaws and teeth. My, what big incisors you have! It is a carnivore.

DEFINITION
A carnivore is a meat eater.

BITE

If the wolverine and a great white shark were the same size, the wolverine would have a stronger jaw.

Great White Shark

FUN FACT
Great white shark teeth are not positioned tightly. They wiggle.

Wolverine

DID YOU KNOW?
Scientists measure jaw strength by "bite force."

STRENGTH

If the Tasmanian devil and a tiger were the same size, the Tasmanian devil would have a stronger bite.

Tiger

AMAZING FACT
Tiger jaws are slightly larger than lion jaws.

Tasmanian Devil

DID YOU KNOW?
The Tasmanian devil has the greatest bite-force ratio of any animal.

FAVORITE FOODS

A wolverine's favorite foods are most animals that live in its area. It eats rabbits, mice, sheep, caribou, lynx, and cows.

FACT

A wolverine is a hunter but is also a scavenger.

rabbit

mouse

sheep

MORE FAVORITE FOODS

Beaver, elk, badgers, otter, voles, dogs, cats, coyotes, squirrels, and chipmunks.

caribou

lynx

cow

DEFINITION

A scavenger is an animal that eats already dead animals.

FAVORITE FOODS

The Tasmanian devil's favorite foods are wombats, possums, and wallabies.

FUN FACT
It also eats kangaroos, wallaroos, sheep, and rabbits.

wombat

wallaby

FULL FACT
A Tasmanian devil can eat almost half its body weight in one sitting.

possum

FACT
It also eats invertebrates such as bugs and moths.

CLAWS

A wolverine has impressive claws. It has no problem digging dens, making snow caves, or shredding logs.

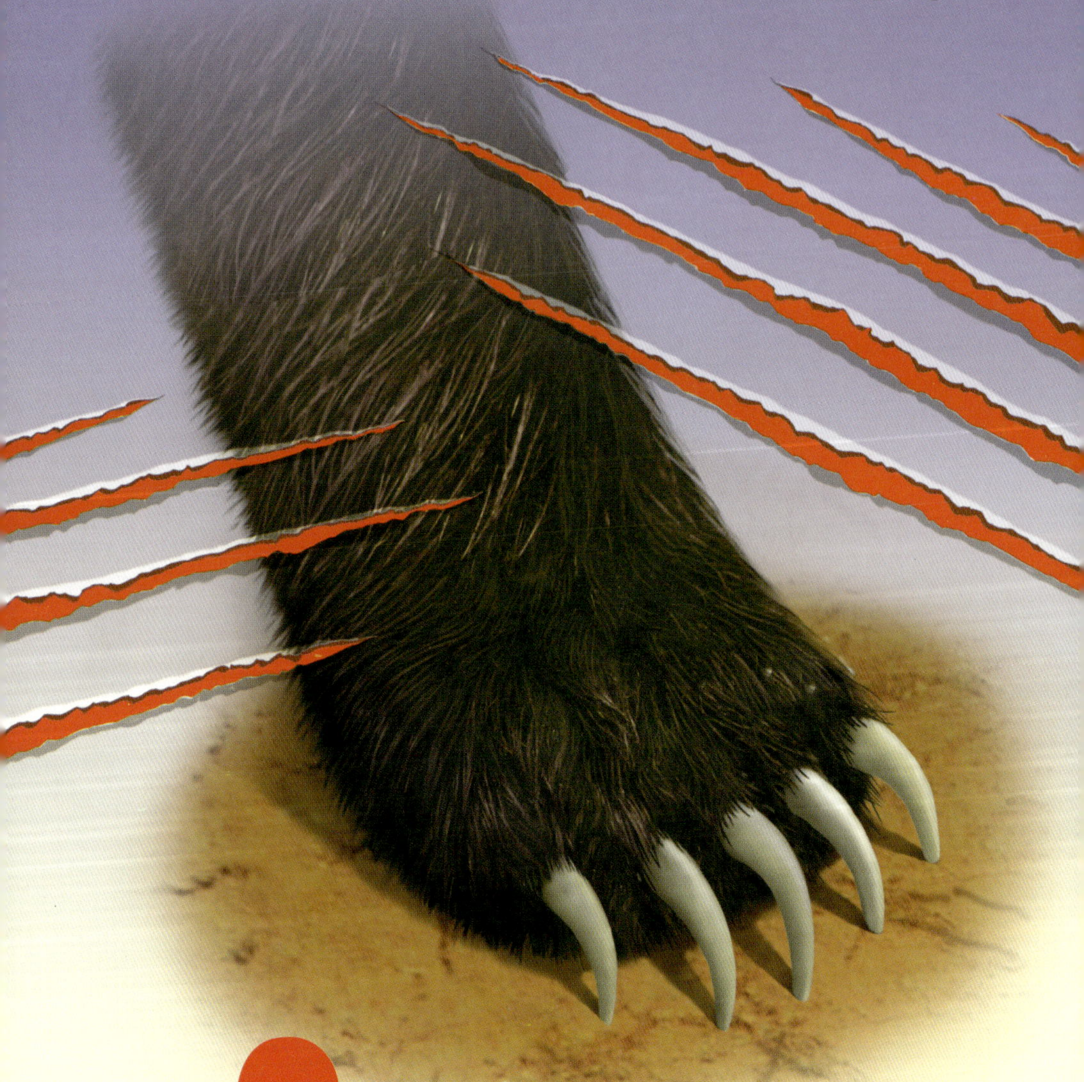

FACT

Even large animals know that a wolverine has deadly claws.

CLAWS

The Tasmanian devil also has long claws that are great for digging. Four claws point forward and one claw points to the side like a thumb. They can pick food up.

DID YOU KNOW?
The Tasmanian devil has only four toes on each hind foot.

FUN FACT
A Tasmanian devil's hind legs are shorter than its front legs.

FUR

In North America, wolverines are a threatened species. Humans have slowly been moving into their territory, and wolverines need a lot of space. Wolverines have been hunted by fur trappers for hundreds of years. They have warm, beautiful fur.

The fur looks like this:

DID YOU KNOW?
Wolverine fur was used for the lining in parkas.

TAIL

CUTE FACT
A baby wolverine is called a kit.

The tail of a wolverine is soft and fluffy. It does not protect it in a fight, but keeps it warm in sub-zero weather.

FUR

Tasmanian devils are also an endangered species. There is no commercial market for Tasmanian devil fur. But Tasmanian devils were hunted for years because they killed animals that fur trappers wanted. They were considered pests.

The fur looks like this:

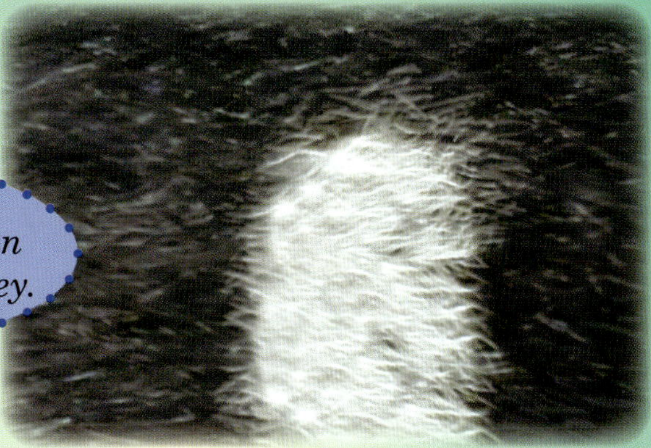

CUTE FACT
A baby Tasmanian devil is called a joey.

The Australian government paid people to kill Tasmanian devils. In 1930, the bounty for a dead Tasmanian devil was 25 cents.

TAIL

DEFINITION
A bounty is money paid for capturing or killing an animal.

FACT
Tasmanian devils have been protected since 1941.

The Tasmanian devil stores fat in its tail. A Tasmanian devil with a skinny tail is an unhealthy animal.

WOLVERINE LEGENDS

BRRR!

In sub-zero weather, a wolverine has no problem climbing up a steep icy mountain.

When tagged by scientists, wolverines were found to be able to hike 80 miles over hilly terrain in one day.

QUESTION?

How long would it take to drive 80 miles if you were traveling at 40 miles per hour?

ANSWER

2 hours.

ONE WOLVERINE CAN MAKE A PACK OF WOLVES RUN AWAY.

Wolverines are so ferocious that scientists only go near them after they have been tranquilized.

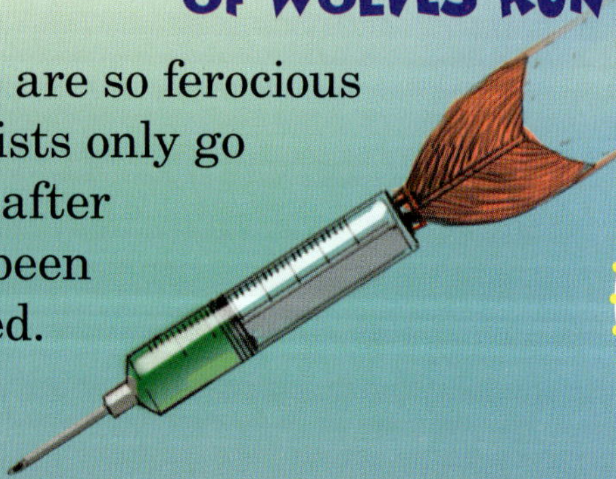

DEFINITION

Tranquilized means drugged by medicine. Zoologists and park rangers shoot drugs instead of bullets to make an animal sleep for a while.

TASMANIAN DEVIL LORE

Their scream has been described as horrifying.

BOOK INTRUDER

The honey badger is mad. Why can't he be in this book? A honey badger can grab a cobra and rip its head off. It would not fear a wolverine or a Tasmanian devil. It wouldn't fear anything!

NAME FACT
The honey badger got its name by fearlessly charging headfirst into African killer bee hives.

DEFINITION
An intruder is someone who goes into a place uninvited.

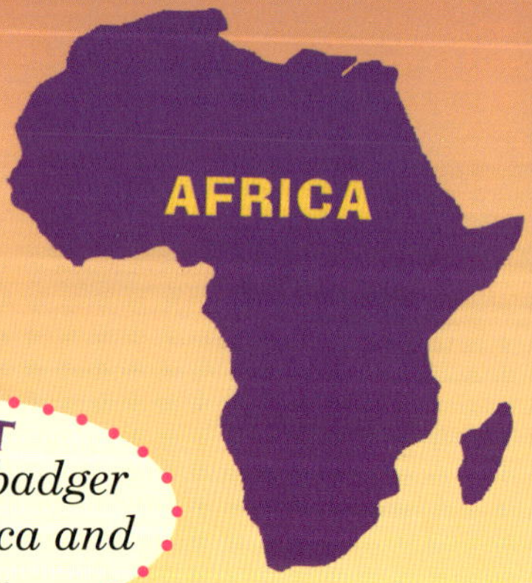

FACT
The honey badger lives in Africa and in Asia.

Should the honey badger get his own book? Which would you prefer reading?

WOLVERINE VS. HONEY BADGER
or
HONEY BADGER VS. TASMANIAN DEVIL

UH-OH! WHO'S THE TOUGHEST?

Three incredible animals! They all look somewhat similar.

In North America the wolverine is considered the toughest animal for its size.

Many people from Australia say that, pound for pound, the Tasmanian devil is the toughest animal in the world. That is quite a compliment, because Australia and Tasmania have some of the most rugged animals on Earth.

People in Africa say that the honey badger is the toughest animal. All three live on different continents. How could they ever meet?

SPEED

A wolverine can run up to 30 miles per hour, which is faster than a human.

TRAP

The safest way to catch a wolverine is with a log-box trap. A chunk of deer is great bait. If you do not check the trap within 24 hours, the wolverine will claw its way out of the trap.

DID YOU KNOW?
A log-box trap doesn't hurt the wolverine.

SPEED

Tasmanian devils can run about 16 miles per hour.

BONUS FACT
A Tasmanian devil can climb a tree, but they prefer not to.

TRAP

The safest way to catch a Tasmanian devil is to set a PVC pipe trap. The Tasmanian devil crawls in to get at the bait. A steak would be great bait.

The wolverine and the Tasmanian devil meet. The Tasmanian devil lets out a scary screech.

The loud noise frightens the wolverine. He takes a step back. The wolverine is puzzled by the Tasmanian devil's scream.

Then the wolverine realizes the Tasmanian devil makes a lot of noise, but takes no action.

He charges at the Tasmanian devil, knocking him down. The wolverine swipes the Tasmanian devil's face.

The Tasmanian devil stops screaming. His face hurts. The wolverine claws at him again. They wrestle back and forth, trying to bite each other.

The wolverine has longer legs and claws. He scratches the Tasmanian devil again. Ouch!

The Tasmanian devil has trouble seeing. The wolverine bites him. The wolverine bites him again and again.

The wolverine wins. This time, the Tasmanian devil is no match for the wolverine.

WHO HAS THE ADVANTAGE?
CHECKLIST

The honey badger is still mad he is not in this book. Can you help him grade these two magnificent animals? Who has the advantage?

WOLVERINE		TASMANIAN DEVIL
☐	**Size**	☐
☐	**Length**	☐
☐	**Jaw strength**	☐
☐	**Voice**	☐
☐	**Fur**	☐
☐	**Claws**	☐

Author note: This is one way the fight might have ended. How would you write the ending?

PAGE 7 ANSWERS:

Quagga: extinct zebra; Quahog: clam; Quail: bird; Quarter horse; Quokka: Australian marsupial; Quoll: marsupial from Australia and New Guinea